MW01596506

HEALING
SCHIZOAFFECTIVE

*A Firsthand Look at the Illness
and How I Beat It!*

JOSHUA ALEXANDER

BALBOA.
PRESS
A DIVISION OF HAY HOUSE

Disclaimer: This book is an account of personal experiences, and the thoughts or opinions expressed herein are not to be taken as a substitute for professional advice. Please consult with a licensed health care practitioner as needed.

Balboa Press books may be ordered through booksellers or by contacting:

Balboa Press
A Division of Hay House
1663 Liberty Drive
Bloomington, IN 47403
www.balboapress.com
1 (877) 407-4847

Because of the dynamic nature of the Internet, any web addresses or links contained in this book may have changed since publication and may no longer be valid. The views expressed in this work are solely those of the author and do not necessarily reflect the views of the publisher, and the publisher hereby disclaims any responsibility for them.

The author of this book does not dispense medical advice or prescribe the use of any technique as a form of treatment for physical, emotional, or medical problems without the advice of a physician, either directly or indirectly. The intent of the author is only to offer information of a general nature to help you in your quest for emotional and spiritual well-being. In the event you use any of the information in this book for yourself, which is your constitutional right, the author and the publisher assume no responsibility for your actions.

Any people depicted in stock imagery provided by Thinkstock are models, and such images are being used for illustrative purposes only. Certain stock imagery © Thinkstock.

Print information available on the last page.

ISBN: 978-1-5043-5363-2 (sc)
ISBN: 978-1-5043-5364-9 (e)

Library of Congress Control Number: 2016904981

Balboa Press rev. date: 05/02/2016

I dedicate this book to my wife, Katherine, who is the light in my life; to my family and friends who supported me throughout my illness; to Dr. Mark Janikula for your devotion to healing people like me; to the caring mental health care workers who were there for me in my time of need; and last but not least, to the One Creator for your endless generosity, love, compassion, and wisdom.

Contents

Introduction

At this point I am enough out of the woods that I feel comfortable telling my story. I have sustained a full-time job for over three years, I am happily married, and I recently bought my first home. I am completely symptom and side-effect free, and for all intents and purposes, I am living a healthy and normal life. In fact, I feel that after having gone through the experience of a debilitating mental illness, I am a better person for it. I am more down-to-earth, humble, caring, and compassionate. My worldview has been reshaped and expanded, and I am more conscious of what really matters in life—and more grateful for it.

It was a decade-long fight, with my first symptoms appearing at age twenty-one, until I finally got off of Social Security disability at age thirty-one. I was first hospitalized in an inpatient unit on the seventh floor, shortly after my twenty-third birthday, and spent Christmas that year in the hospital. I was diagnosed with schizoaffective disorder. At the time, I thought some of the nurses were aliens living among us to help us evolve. The National Alliance on Mental Illness (NAMI) website describes Schizoaffective disorder as follows:

"Schizoaffective disorder is a serious mental illness that affects about one in 100 people. Schizoaffective disorder as a diagnostic entity has features that resemble both schizophrenia and also serious mood (affective) symptoms." (http://www.nami.org)

One in a hundred people doesn't seem like a lot (and some estimates put it at one in two hundred), but if you take the US population in 2013 of 316 million, that would mean that around 3.16 million people in the United States alone could have schizoaffective disorder. That's a lot of people, and that's just one form of mental illness. (Schizoaffective disorder is actually less common than schizophrenia!) What's unfortunate is that many people with mental illness are not able to advocate for themselves, do not have the resources available to meet their needs, and are still subject to stigma and blame around their illness, although awareness around this issue is rising.

The aspect of schizoaffective disorder that resembles schizophrenia—the psychotic symptoms—can be hallucinations, delusions, and/or other symptoms of a thought disorder, such as negative symptoms. In terms of the mood symptoms, there are two types: depressive or bipolar. I have thought of it as kind of a hybrid between schizophrenia and a mood disorder. I had the depressive type, and my psychotic symptoms included various delusions, visual, olfactory and sensory hallucinations, and negative symptoms such as flat affect. Luckily for me I did not have auditory hallucinations, which I can imagine would be very disturbing to experience.

One of the more difficult lessons that I learned during the early years of my illness was that the illness is a real thing. When my psychotic symptoms would come on, they seemed like an extension of my normal experiences, and like many people, I did not have a strong awareness that I was sick. I knew or had read about people who had similar thoughts or experiences to my "symptoms," and they were leading normal, even successful lives. I thought that I just had heightened perceptions, and that I could sense things that other people couldn't. After all, the "diagnosis" is made based on matching patient reports and doctor observations with a few criteria in a book. It is not as black and white as a broken bone, something that can be seen with diagnostic tools and measured.

It wasn't until after my first major relapse that landed me back up on the seventh floor that I realized the illness was real. I had tried everything in my power to stay well: healthy eating, exercise, social integration, a structured schedule, and psychotherapy. I had given it all I had, and I still ended up back in the hospital. I felt incredibly powerless to change my situation. It felt like a black hole, and—like light that cannot escape its gravity—no matter how strong I was, I could not escape. I was unable to hold down a job, take care of myself, socialize normally, or lead a normal life in any way, shape, or form.

At one point (I think during the inpatient stay after my first relapse), my perspective on the illness shifted. I stopped questioning whether or not the symptoms were real and started looking at the illness as an inability to function in my life. That fact, that I could not make my life work, was what I began to see as the illness. This simple shift in perspective created a tremendous sense of relief for me, and I felt a newfound acceptance of my situation. I now had an opponent, something to fight. My mission would be to regain functioning in my life, and I would pull out all the stops.

Part of what made it so hard for me, and what was probably also a blessing, was that I still felt like myself throughout the whole experience. Inside, it still felt like me. I did not feel ill deep down inside, but my experience of the world was very altered. It was like living inside a Stanley Kubrick film, where the world is scary and does not make sense.

At that time, I also started to look at the illness as more of a brain disorder. My mind (or my inner awareness) seemed to still be working as it always had, but the data it was being fed—and its interpretation of it—was all garbled. A couple of times I realized that some of my delusions stemmed from my mind trying to process such a fragmented experience of reality. It was like my mind was filling in the gaps in my experience, and some of the thoughts that had "bridged" the gaps were my delusions.

At that time, I made a decision to let go of any resistance or rigid beliefs that I had around my recovery. I would utilize all of the resources at my disposal, even medication (which I was strongly opposed to), to get better. I was going to get back on my feet and get my power back, so that I was not at the mercy of the illness or my situation. I was going to beat it!

After the first few sections of this book, I am going to include a few poems that I wrote during that time period, to give you a sense of how I was thinking and feeling at the time, as well as photos of myself (for visual effect).

The following are some poems that I wrote in 2001, about a year before my first symptoms appeared:

Poems (2001)

Constant Existence
Love is not something to be gained or lost
Watch how the sun melts the morning frost
Watch closely, for its existence is there
Love warms your skin so do not despair

(July 23, 2001)

Innate Knowledge
I believe the answer lies within
It is inherent in all life, in a tree,
A cat, a worm, in all matter;
You can see it in the sidewalk
Sometimes you feel it when you're sleeping,
In the instant you realize you're awake
It is present in a lover's kiss
Staring in her eyes or at the starlit sky;
It's not different
Love is there. It is rich with Energy.
And yet I am blind
Every now and then I feel a glimpse of light

Light powerful enough to bring hope
The desire to continue, to love, to breathe,
To exist
For though I cannot see it,
I know it is there.

(July 23, 2001)

Self-Pact
If the pain is unbearable
If things don't go my way
If I think I'm not able
If my thoughts are astray

If my desires overcome me
If I feel depressed
If there's something I can't see
If I'm not at my best

If I have to give it all I've got
If I'm afraid I will fall
If I want to be someone I'm not
If I don't want anything at all

If I realize I've been wrong
If the battle is lost
If I don't feel very strong
If I can't pay the cost

If I want something really bad
If I've fallen from above
If I forget to feel glad

If I can't feel the love

Even if I don't know why not to quit
The reason has slipped my mind, or it just doesn't fit
In the name of the little boy who
once stared at the world
With eyes full of wonder, who took what was hurled
Who believed in justice, and whose love was so pure
I don't know much, but I do know for sure
I will never give up

(October 26, 2001)

*A healthy college-aged young adult, ready for
my first time water-skiing; Summer 2001.*

GETTING SICK

Onset of My First Symptoms

During my last year of undergraduate school at Cornell University, I became a different person than I had ever been before. Cornell had been a nearly insurmountable challenge for me, and during the majority of it, I had fantasized about dropping out and sailing around the world, taking a motorcycle trip to South America, opening an avocado farm, or undertaking some other wild and free adventure. The first semester of my senior year, I studied abroad in Argentina. I lived with a host family, attended the local university, had an Argentinean girlfriend, and traveled to Chile and Uruguay. People say that traveling can expand your worldview or cause culture shock, but I didn't really believe it or understand it until I experienced it for myself.

My semester in Argentina opened my eyes to a whole different world. It expanded me in ways that I had never known were possible, and I grew as a human being. Upon returning to Cornell for my last semester that winter, I decided that I was going to live my best life. I was going to do something meaningful, something that I was passionate about. I was pretty burned out from school at that point, so I decided to take a year off after graduation, do some more traveling, and maybe teach yoga and meditation. Little did I know that things don't always work out the way they are planned.

When I left home after high school, I was one type of person. I had been domesticated by my family, by the area of the world I grew up in, by my teachers, and by the environment around me. When I came home after college, I was a completely different person. I had grown in ways I could never have imagined. My worldview had expanded. I had known pleasures and pains that I had only read about in storybooks.

My childhood home and my family were exactly the same as they were when I left. The contrast and shock that I experienced when moving back home were almost unbearable. My parents were not in favor of me taking time off before getting a job or going to graduate school. Their belief systems were the same, in line with the way that I had thought before college—but not after. I felt misunderstood and controlled. I was angry, and needless to say, this created a lot of friction between me and my family.

As part of my desire to "live meaningfully," I had adopted a vegan diet the month before graduation. That was also something that my parents disagreed with. The more they tried to control my diet, the more I clung to it.

I needed to be free, to be my own person. My plan was to work and save up enough money to travel somewhere, practice yoga, and follow my passion. That summer, I got a job as a waiter at a fancy restaurant and as a filing clerk at a law firm during the day. All would have been well, except that I didn't feel well. I was absolutely exhausted, and I felt a terrible weight in my being. Everything was an effort. I attributed this to my burnout from Cornell, but people told me it shouldn't take that long to recover. As far as I was concerned, it could have taken five years to recover. I felt that I needed rest and healing on a deep level.

During that time, I started to let my mind wander into expansive thoughts about life, the universe, and the nature of reality. Some days I would lie on my bedroom floor and stare up at the ceiling for hours. Somehow my desire for freedom turned into a feeling of powerlessness, of being trapped. I felt like I didn't have the energy to fulfill my dreams. I was losing weight from my overly-restrictive diet and from the stress and conflict I was under—and the isolation. I was fighting with my family, and I was spiraling downward.

That fall of 2002, during a weeklong volunteer stay at a retreat center, things turned for the worse. I was having trouble sleeping, and I started to feel things that weren't normal. One night I felt like my body was becoming permeable to my surroundings, as if there were no boundary between me and the outside world. (Just to note, I was not doing drugs at this time. I had only smoked marijuana about eighteen times during my freshman year in college, which was nearly three and a half years prior to this point.)

I got up and stared at myself in the mirror. I felt as if a wind were blowing across and through my body. I began breathing rapidly through sheer panic. My thoughts were running wild. I would calm myself down and slow my breathing to a point where I felt okay, but then the panic would return and I would be almost hyperventilating. This happened a couple of times—my breathing speeding up and then slowing down—and I thought, *I am Cheyne-Stoking.* I had once seen someone do that on their death bed before dying. At that point, I just lost it.

A Taste of People Looking at Me Differently

The next day I was in a complete daze. I was so unpresent and ungrounded that I missed a scheduled meal. I began to feel even more ungrounded, so I went to the kitchen and asked for some food. The kitchen staff was kind of rude to me, saying that I had to eat during mealtimes, and I just burst into tears. The woman from the kitchen then brought me a peanut butter sandwich, which I began eating, but at that point I just started to move into panic again.

I tried to find the volunteer program coordinator for help, but when I found her she just said, "You'd better be careful. They locked my family member up and they threw away the key. You'd better get help." I felt hurt by this and struck by fear. I had been talking to another volunteer that week about how I felt I couldn't "bridge the gap" between where I was in my life and where I wanted to be, and she had responded with, "Did you ever think that you may have a mental illness?" That deeply angered me, because I had felt pretty normal (aside from the fatigue and low energy) up until that point.

I talked to the volunteer program coordinator again, and we decided it would be best if I shortened my stay, so I left the week-long volunteer stint about two days early. This was the first time I had bailed out on a commitment in my life, but it would not be the last. Unfortunately, this would become a pattern for me over the next decade. When I got home, I agreed to talk to a therapist.

My dad set me up with a therapist who I thought would understand me, because she was a little more progressive. She was into health food and spirituality. I met with her a few times, but it didn't really seem to be helping. I decided to stop seeing her and handle my struggles on my own. Around that time, the friction at home had been increasing, and I was not getting along with my mother. I had lost a lot of weight, and she was worried about me.

I had been blaming my parents for trying to control me and not letting me be *me*. My mother came up to me one day and said, "You have a mental illness." I was so infuriated that I lost control. I shoved her and started screaming, "F-ck you! F-ck you!" over and over again right in her face at the top of my lungs. She started smashing me in the face with her palms and screaming at me over and over again.

Thankfully, someone started knocking at the front door, which was enough to end the incident. I immediately went to my room and started packing my things. I had this really cool Jeep Cherokee at the time, and I loaded it up and started driving to Ithaca, New York, where I had gone to college. I really liked that town and didn't feel that I had enjoyed it while I was there, since I had spent most of my time in one of the nine college libraries on campus. On the drive there, I called a friend who had gone to Cornell with me and whose family lived in Ithaca, and he let me stay on his sofa that night.

The next day I started out building a life for myself, or so I had planned. Ironically, at that time, I wanted to get involved in helping people with mental illnesses, even though it would be a decade before I was well enough to take care of myself. I applied for a position with AmeriCorps at the local mental health organization. It was like a volunteer position, but I would get a stipend to cover my living expenses.

I was also trying to get involved in the local community. I remember searching, walking around town, and looking up online groups or organizations that I could be a part of. I even talked to random people on the street a couple of times. It seemed that as hard as I tried, I could not form any connections or relationships. I believe that my desperation was part of the problem. People don't like forming connections with others who have "needy energy." It began to look as if my plan to build a new life for myself in Ithaca was turning into a complete failure.

The Hospital Visit from Hell

Additionally, my symptoms were worsening. One morning I walked downtown to go to a coffee shop. It was wet out from raining overnight, and I was walking through the grass in a town park. It felt as if my body was permeable to the outside world again, like the environment was going right through me. The grass was wet, and I thought I could feel the water moving right through my feet. These experiences were quite scary and caused me to feel panicked. I'm not sure how long after that I was having intense burning in my stomach from the anxiety.

One evening it was getting so bad that I drove to the grocery store to try to find something that would help me. For some reason I thought that drinking milk would help. I thought that it was a base and that it would counteract the acid in my stomach. I went into the grocery store and grabbed a carton of milk off the shelf, and my stomach was burning so badly that I just opened it right there in the store and took a swig. I immediately vomited right on the floor in the aisle. At that point I was losing control, so I rapidly walked up to the payphone at the front of the store (they still had those in 2003) and called 911. An ambulance came and took me to the hospital.

The panic and anxiety was literally so bad that I lost consciousness in the ambulance on the way to the hospital (either that or I was given a sedative). The last thing I remember was my arm hanging limp and bending over the sidebar of the stretcher as the EMT put a needle into it. I awoke to the sound of a nurse trying to get an elderly woman to take a drink in a neighboring room. The nurse kept saying "swallow" over and over again slowly in this creepy way, and I could hear the choking and gurgling sound of the patient. It was really freaky. Everything seemed as if it were a dream, happening slowly and deliberately, and in a scary way.

When it was my turn, the nurse came to the side of my bed. She looked pale and pasty like a ghost, and I had a thought that she was dead or something. She began injecting something into the IV in my arm, and whatever substance was coming in through the tube was burning my arm badly. I had remembered someone saying that you're not supposed to put an IV into an artery, and I wondered if that was the case then. I told the nurse that it was burning, but she didn't do anything about it. I remember feeling scared, helpless, and alone, as though the people around me didn't see me and weren't conscious or considerate of my feelings. I felt so physically ill that I asked the nurse if she thought I had cancer. She just shrugged it off, as if I were crazy.

When the nurse left, the IV was burning so badly, and I was so scared that I began calling for her. I yelled "Nurse! Nurse!" a few times, but no one came. At that point, I pulled the IV out of my arm, and blood and fluid spurted out onto the floor. I squeezed the clamp on the tube of the IV to stop the flow of liquid, and headed out of the room to a bathroom to clean up my arm. I threw up again onto the floor at the entrance of the bathroom, partly from the burning in my stomach and partly from the extreme anxiety of the experience.

Someone came and escorted me back to my room, and when the doctor came in to talk to me, he was even scarier than the nurse. He looked like he hadn't slept in days, had bags under his eyes, and his eyes kind of rolled back and to the side of his head when he talked. He looked like a zombie, or at least like he was on some of the drugs he was prescribing. Again, it was like he didn't even see me and was just saying things he had memorized, or like he was reciting from a book.

He told me that there was blood in my vomit. I said, "No there's not. It's brown," and it seemed to anger him that I had questioned his authority. With an irritated tone, he repeated, "Yes, there is. There's a discoloration." He started to put on latex gloves and said that he had to do a rectal exam to see if there was blood in my stool. That didn't seem like a normal thing to do to me, and my panic increased a few notches. I told him that I didn't consent to that, and I was relieved that he didn't push the issue. When he left the room, I was in absolute terror. I didn't feel safe in the hands of these people, and I didn't trust them.

The next person who came to see me was a representative from the local mental health authority. When she talked to me, I got the feeling that she was mentally unstable, and the fact that she was questioning my mental health really topped off the terror I was feeling. I quickly walked down the hall to the nurses' station and found the doctor sitting there. I asked him if I could leave. He snapped, "We were here for you. Now you wait for us." I couldn't believe that he was actually unaware of how much pain I was feeling. I felt like I could burst into tears.

He wrote a prescription for who knows what and handed it to me. I walked toward the exit, dropping the prescription into the trash can as I left. Now, the hospital was a few miles from town, and my car was still back at the grocery store on the opposite side of town, where I had been picked up by the ambulance. It was very early in the morning, and not knowing what to do, I started walking down the road.

I remember feeling so weak, sick to my stomach, and physically ill that I didn't know how I would make the walk. My intense fear was the only thing keeping me going at that point. I was about halfway to town when a police cruiser pulled up beside me. Thankfully, he told me he would give me a lift and drove me back to the center of town. I was still a few miles away from my car, so I just walked back to my apartment and curled up in bed.

Back to the Nest

At this point, while I didn't think that I had a mental illness, I knew that I was not okay. I did what most people do in that situation: I called my parents. It's funny how we get angry at them and blame them for anything and everything, but they are the first people we call when we are in real trouble. I called my father (who has bailed me out of trouble more times than I can count), and he literally dropped everything and started the five-hour drive to Ithaca to pick me up. He picked me up and took me back to Connecticut. His girlfriend was kind enough to let me move in with them at her house.

I had lost a lot of weight at this point because I was restricting what I was eating due to the fact that I could "feel" the energy of my food. My mood would shift dramatically based on what I ate, so I was being very rigid about food and being overly selective about it. I remember conflict at the dinner table created by my selectivity around food. This loss of weight was likely not helping my physical or mental state.

My father decided to schedule an appointment for me with a general practitioner. When we got to the doctor's office for my appointment, the office staff looked extremely unhealthy, and I had that same fearful feeling that I had gotten at the hospital in Ithaca. The staff looked either morbidly obese or sickly thin. They were pale and pasty, and I questioned if they were alive. The doctor was more of the thin type, but I could tell that she was kind and really cared. She did an exam and then told me that I may need antidepressants.

For the most part, I was not actually feeling depressed. She said she thought it had gone too far by that point. She advised me that I needed more calories and to eat anything I wanted, even ice cream, chips, or whatever. I was adamantly against medication, so I refused the antidepressants, but I did try eating as she prescribed. The problem was, I would eat a bowl of ice cream, and my mood would shift dramatically. My body would feel heavy, and I would feel depressed. Other foods would shift how I felt in other ways.

I spent the summer of 2003 living there with my dad and his girlfriend. I volunteered at an organic farm, took yoga classes, and tried to get involved. I did not want to be isolated like before, which I didn't think was good for me, and I wanted to live my life. At the end of the summer, I ended up having a dispute with my dad and his girlfriend over what I thought was a trivial matter, but they disagreed, and I decided to leave (which was starting to become a pattern with me).

Ironically, I moved back in with my mother. I don't remember much from that autumn, but that December was the first time that I was admitted into an inpatient facility. I was on a family trip to New York City for our annual holiday party, and my symptoms were full blown. I thought that I was breathing in my great uncle's cancer, unintentionally controlling other people with my energy, and much more. It took all of my strength to hold myself together and pretend like nothing was wrong. I was feeling and experiencing things that were terrifying to me, but I didn't know what to do or how to change it.

First Inpatient Stay

When the ambulance came, I was selectively catatonic. I don't remember the ambulance ride, but I woke up in a hospital bed with harried and concerned people standing over me. I thought of the scene from *The Matrix* when Neo first wakes up in the pod in the real world. I thought something like that was happening. I started to feel fear again, so I asked for my parents. I said it again with emphasis: "I want to see my parents," and one of the nurses stopped and said "Okay." My parents came into the room, and my mother was crying. I had lost so much weight that my ribs were showing. Normally a 210-pound person, I weighed in around 145 pounds. I remember someone saying that I looked like a holocaust victim.

After that, a very caring mental health representative came to talk to me. I was sent up to the seventh floor for the first time. When I got there, one of the nurses came up to me and looked right at me. Whereas I felt like most of the time other people weren't really aware of me, this nurse was present—as if she could actually see me—and she talked directly to me. It was so unusual that I was shocked. I thought that maybe she was an alien living among us to help us evolve. I felt heard and safe for the first time in a while.

I was in the hospital for ten days that stay, and I spent Christmas of 2003 in there. I guess something about psychotic breaks make people constipated—or maybe it was being on the new medication—but I didn't have a bowel movement until day seven. Needless to say, it was painful! I was put on Paxil for the depression and Risperdal, which they said would help me sleep. I don't remember much else from that stay, but when I was given my discharge papers to sign on day ten, I noticed that it said my diagnosis was "Schizoaffective Disorder." That was the first I had heard of it, and I was upset that no one had told me.

I went up to the nurse who had first greeted me on the seventh floor and told her I felt lied to. She apologized. I told her that I had been lying too, and that I thought there were aliens living among us (although I didn't tell her that I thought she was one). She said that she had some odd beliefs too, as do other people. I told her that I didn't want to get onto the government system (Medicare, disability, and so on), and she said that if I did, it would be possible for me to get off of it. I signed the discharge papers and was released into the partial-hospital program.

Throughout the partial-hospital program, I was still coming down from my psychotic high. I was also still having intense energy experiences around food and feeling hypersensitive around other people. The partial-hospital program was like being in a support group for most of the day for a few days a week, and at the very least it gave me structure and someplace to go. I felt like it was a game, and I had to learn how to behave and act. I would try to look for cues and clues from other people, to figure out how I should behave. I felt like other people were in on something that I was unaware of, and I was just playing along.

After the partial-hospital program ended and I was at home with nothing to do, a depression like I had never experienced before started to set in. They call it *post-psychotic depression*, and it felt like my body weighed a thousand pounds. I felt like I was full of lead, and my mood was at rock bottom. My mind was dull, as were my emotions, and physically I had no energy. I was so low that I could barely move. I couldn't believe it.

I blamed the medications for giving me a "chemical lobotomy" and causing me to feel so depressed. After a few weeks, I had another inpatient stay for a medication adjustment (which would not be the last time), and the Paxil was switched to Effexor. After that, the Risperdal was switched to Zyprexa. Eventually, I was put on Zoloft and Abilify. Riding the rollercoaster of med changes is no fun at all. It is excruciatingly slow and painful and feels like a guessing game. I seemed to be doing okay on the Zoloft and Abilify and ended up staying on those for a while. As someone described to me, "The medication puts the floor back underneath you." While I was starting to be able to function, I would hardly say that it was "living."

These poems were from 2002 to 2003 when my symptoms appeared but before I was diagnosed:

Poems (2002 – 2003)

Thought

As I wake from a dark slumber
A question comes to my mind
Where have I been I wonder
I've been here all the time

(April 29, 2002)

Stone Edifice

Constructed around
One will find
Confusion abounds
Imposed on the mind

Given a brick
Built pure from scratch
One stands outside
By the door's open latch

(May 18, 2002)

Stand Tall

Breaking Point
Growing heavier
Until one drops the load

Fear of the fall
Trying to stand tall

(June 17, 2002)

Journey
Traveling along the path
In silent exploration,
Content with each step,
Soul slowly blossoming
Filling with warmth,
Opening to the possible

(July 1, 2002)

Why
Independent souls traveling free
Choosing who we want to be
Always eating of the apple tree

Do we need a reason why?
Why to live and not to die?
Why to love or why to cry?

A drummist plays, plays his drum
He doesn't ask where it comes from
Life is here, partake of some.

Each moment, a chance to revere
Each of us, our own seer
Running water, is much more clear

Stop searching, and start living
Stop trying, and start being
Stop questioning, and start believing.

(November 25, 2002)

I Cannot Tell

There is something moving inside me
Do I want to silence it or feed it?
I cannot tell.
This longing for longing
I want to burn and sweat and ache
I pray only that I do not turn away
Oh this aching to feel an ache
An echo of something that has once been,
Or something that has yet to come
I cannot tell.
I pray only that I do not turn away
That I stay with it and seek it out
This endless journey
Self-fulfilled by nature
A search to seek
Suspended in time
Pulsating beauty
As if time itself is breathing
Is it me that is stretching or the world?
To hold this, to seek this
If only I could share this
What is it that I want?
I cannot tell.

(July 17, 2003)

The day before my first inpatient hospitalization, weighing in around 145 pounds; December 2003.

A DECADE WITH MENTAL ILLNESS, PART I

The Long and Winding Road

It was spring of 2004, and I got a job working in a warehouse picking items for shipping. I was slotted to work ten hours per week, but I did not have a set schedule and could come in whenever I chose. Due to how I was feeling, it was very challenging for me to go in and stay in. I would pack a lunch and start driving there, and I was so anxious that I would eat my lunch in the car on my way to work. Eating was one of my negative coping mechanisms at the time, and I would eat when I was anxious, for comfort. Once there, I would usually only stay for a little while, maybe an hour. After a short period of time, I stopped going.

A childhood friend of mine was back home after graduating college, and I talked to him about my situation and how I was having such a hard time. He didn't have any plans for the summer, so we decided to apply to be camp counselors together. We got a job for eight weeks at a nearby sleepaway camp. I remember how difficult that summer was for me. From about 7 a.m. when the kids got up until 9 p.m. when they went to bed, I not only had to usher them around and keep them engaged but also I was responsible for leading a few activities each day. These were group activities in different fields—in sports, arts and crafts, or whatever.

I was so exhausted every day all day that I constantly had to push myself. I remember feeling that just walking from one place of the camp to another took an enormous amount of energy, as if I were walking through thigh-high mud. I had to force myself to take each step. In addition to the low energy, I had a dull feeling mentally from the medication. I felt numb behind my forehead, like the front of my brain was anesthetized. It was a miserable eight weeks, and I don't know how I made it through it. I know that I could not have done it if my friend hadn't been there for support.

After that summer, I decided to stop taking the Abilify. I couldn't bear the low energy and mental dullness any longer. Around that time, my mother had encouraged me to apply for Social Security disability. I didn't really want to do it, because I didn't want to accept that I couldn't take care of myself, and I didn't want to be dependent on the system. She helped me fill out the application, and I was accepted. It turns out that it was a lifesaver, because there were many times over the next few years that I depended on the disability income to survive. At that point, the monthly check was around $400. It was not enough to live on, but it helped.

I decided to move to Boston with the friend that I had worked at the camp with, and I tried to make a life for myself there. It was a three- to four-bedroom apartment, and one of the rooms—the one that I took—was more like a large closet. My roommates decided to divide up the rent based on room-size, so I only had to pay around $275 a month. I knew that I could cover that with my disability income, even if I couldn't maintain work.

I tried working at a crepe cafe for a little while, and that didn't work out, so I tried to come up with another plan. I had always done well in school, so I was considering going to graduate school. One of my main passions is natural health, and my father is a chiropractor, so I thought that I could become a chiropractor and work with him. I gathered all of the paperwork necessary, applied to chiropractic college, and was accepted. In early 2005, I loaded up my beloved Jeep and drove down to Georgia to attend school. I also decided to go off the Zoloft, because I didn't really believe in medication, and if I were to be a natural doctor, I thought that I didn't want to be a hypocrite and be on medication.

That first quarter at chiropractic school I felt like myself again for the first time since my illness had started. It was like I was back "on fire," like my Cornell days, except that I was more excited about what I was learning because it was something practical that I would be using for work. I was active and involved in numerous activities, such as volunteering at the school fundraising office, going to the gym regularly, and starting a club. I was making friends and was doing great. That first quarter I got a 4.0 GPA. I was back to myself again.

My First Relapse

Around the beginning of the second quarter, an acquaintance that I had met at a school function came knocking at my roommates' and my door one evening. She was saying things that didn't make sense, like that we needed to help her break some glass. After our startled reaction subsided, I realized that she wasn't thinking clearly. I told my roommates that I would handle it and walked her back to her apartment. I thought that because I had been through psychosis, I could help her. I naively thought that I could talk her down from it.

We sat at her kitchen table, and she told me she wanted me to call her by a different name (like a theme from the movie *The Neverending Story*). She was upset and said, "I don't understand why you won't just call me by this name." I told her that I wouldn't, because I didn't believe it mattered what I called her (and I didn't want to enable her delusion). Her behavior seemed to be getting worse, not better, and she said she was hearing voices.

I was starting to feel out of control, so I left to go get a friend. I told him to stay with her for a little while and make sure she was okay. I didn't think to get a doctor, because I felt I had been so hurt by doctors and western medicine that I didn't think it would help her, and I didn't see it as the right solution.

Leading up to this point, I had had some funny symptoms return. I was starting to feel more sensitive, and I remember eating a spoonful of peanut butter and feeling like I was being pulled into it. After the incident with this girl, I quickly spiraled out of control. Within a couple of days, I was having a difficult time maintaining my schedule and making it to my classes. I remember walking around the campus at night and throwing all of my expensive textbooks into a dumpster.

I had been talking with the school counselor all along, because I wanted to maintain my mental health while at school. I called her, and she advised me to get to a hospital. It was a private mental health facility near the school, and my roommate drove me there. At the time, I thought it was a school for the gifted or for people with special powers, like Xavier's School in *The X-Men* comic.

The staff brought me into an observation room before being admitted, and I thought it was some type of test. There was a sofa and a desk with some computer parts and a swivel chair. I looked around trying to figure out what I was supposed to do. My mind was being pulled in all different directions by conflicting, incongruent thoughts.

I was so tormented inside that my body was jolting around. I was doing everything in my power to hold myself together. After a short time, one of the staff members came into the room and told me that I didn't meet the criteria for admittance. After he left the room, I stood there with my body stiff and my hands on a table looking at their brochure, which read, "It's hard enough to ask for help; it shouldn't be hard to get it." Ironically, I was finding it very hard to get the help I needed in my life. (I should note that it was an exceptional facility, and I think it was a misunderstanding—not their unwillingness to help me by admitting me.)

I felt that I had failed in some way, and I felt hurt by life that I couldn't find help. I felt that I had given all I had to give and was defeated. I lay down on the sofa and completely surrendered. I completely gave up and let go. I curled up into a ball and felt myself absorbing into myself, my awareness closing in. I thought that I was dying and was okay with it, and I immediately thought about my family and how hurt they would feel if I passed. I started seeing images from my childhood flash before my eyes, like the life-reel that people reportedly see before they die.

I felt like I was being wrapped in a warm blanket and was being absorbed. It actually felt quite comforting. At that moment, the door burst open and the staff member rushed in and said, "Okay, we'll admit you." The shock startled me out of what I was experiencing, and I gasped for breath, making the sound that I thought a ghost would make. My mom later told me that the staff at the hospital had told her that they had admitted me due to an emergency. I know people say you can't die from a mental illness, but I felt I came fairly close that night.

While in the inpatient unit, I was in a really bad way. I was very hypersensitive, like I was on an extreme adrenaline-high. I remember filling out the intake form that asked if my condition was psychological, and/or related to addiction (some people have what they call a "dual-diagnosis" for a mental illness and an addiction), and I wrote "psych-addict." That's how I felt at the time, as if my thoughts had sped off on their own, and I couldn't slow them down or diffuse them.

During that inpatient stay as well, I thought that some of the nurses were aliens. I thought they were aware of the things that I was aware of. I was constantly trying to do everything right, as if I were trying to figure out the "rules." There was a bulletin board on the wall in the main room with a calendar and some ground rules for the inpatient unit. I was trying to study them, so I could follow them to a tee, but I was having difficulty making sense of them.

I remember in one of the group sessions, a woman was staring at me, and I thought that she was helping me to stay focused with her mind. Needless to say, I was in bad shape. I felt physically frail and weak, like how it must feel being close to death. Later that day, that same woman who had been staring at me at the group session offered me a couple of dollars for the vending machine, and I quickly turned it down. In my extreme interpretation of karma, I didn't want to take anything that I hadn't earned and create an imbalance.

I think I was discharged on the fifth day, and a friend of the family who lived in the area picked me up and brought me to his home. He very generously let me stay there with his family for a couple of days. It was a few weeks into the second quarter of school, and I determined that I couldn't continue, so my mom decided to drive down to Georgia to pick me up. I had racked up $15,000 in student loan debt by this point and was now back on medication with no plan for my future. I had also signed over my $6,000 jeep to my roommate's mother for nothing. The radiator had broken and the car had been towed, and I told her that she could have it if she paid to get it out of the tow lot and to fix the radiator. This was also part of my tendency to give away my material possessions when I was sick. I loved that jeep, and that choice hurt for years afterwards.

Basically, after all of my effort over the previous year and a half to get back on my feet, I would now have to start over again from scratch. Part of what made my illness so difficult was not only the physical and mental pain but also the incredible losses I endured. In addition to the material losses, I lost relationships, my identity, and my trust in life (which I have subsequently regained). On the plus side, suffering is a powerful way of disintegrating the ego, and I feel that I have grown tremendously as a human being from the experience and am now a much better person for it. I am much more compassionate and focused on what really matters. Every day I am grateful for the blessings I have and the simple things in my life that most people take for granted—but that I had once lost.

When my mother arrived, we packed what we could fit of my personal belongings into my mother's car, and started the seventeen-hour drive home. Though I had been discharged from the hospital, I was still in somewhat of a psychotic state. I did my best to hold it together during that car ride, but I was experiencing intense anxiety which made the trip very challenging for me. My mother is one of the strongest people I have ever met. She doesn't even like leaving her home, or traveling at all, and she drove seventeen hours to pick me up.

She's also very stubborn and doesn't care what other people think. (While there are some drawbacks to this quality, it can also have a positive effect on self-worth, by not defining yourself by what other people think of you.)

While she sometimes comes off as intense to other people because of these traits, I attribute some of my ability to overcome the illness to these qualities that I inherited from her. When we arrived home that first night, I was still having trouble sleeping. During my acute psychotic breaks, my sleep was one of the main things that was affected. My thoughts were still running out of control, and I was still experiencing intense anxiety and fear. I woke my mother up, and we determined that I had to go back into the hospital. It was the summer of 2005.

Rebuilding My Life Again

For me, a relapse of my mental illness was like getting into a motorcycle accident and needing extensive rehabilitation. Most of the work that I had done—at least in terms of what was externally visible—was destroyed, and I would have to start over. I was left in a physically weakened state. All of the work in applying to school, moving to a new state, and studying that first quarter of school was now useless. I was back at home without a job, without a schedule, and without a plan. I had actually enjoying being back at school, and had felt for a short while that my life was working again.

Now, back up on the seventh floor, I was once again lost in the world. My parents had and have always been there to "bail me out" when I was in trouble. They were like a safety net, in case I fell too far. At this point, they had been deeply affected by my illness as well. Mental illness can put incredible strain on family members, and I know it was not easy for them, either.

Normally, they would have let me move back in with one of them at home, but this time, they wanted to try tough love. I guess they were thinking that if I faced conditions that were uncomfortable enough, I would be motivated to change my situation. Also, it was putting considerable strain on my stepparents—and potentially their relationships. What I don't think they realized was that I was already giving it everything I had. I was giving it my all and trying my best, but I was still failing.

Since my parents were not going to let me move back home, I met with a social worker at the inpatient unit. I was given the choice between going to the local homeless "Fish" shelter after discharge or to a local group home for the mentally ill. I had often thought about the prospects of being homeless and sometimes even romanticized it, as if I would be some type of martyr who didn't fit into society and could feel sorry for myself for being a victim of society's injustices.

However, I knew that I did not have the courage to be homeless and that the pain would be unbearable to me. Therefore, I chose to go to the group home. When I got there, it was explained to me that they would be collecting my Social Security disability directly to pay for my stay, administer my medications, and that I was required to attend random, unscheduled meetings throughout the day. This last requirement precluded me from getting a job. I quickly realized that this was not a stepping-stone to a normal functioning life, but rather a rest home.

I was absolutely miserable there. Even when I was broke, living off of my disability and some part-time income (basically at the poverty line), I was buying organic health food. I never bought new clothes or other things people buy, but health food is one of my main passions. The food at the group home made the SAD (Standard American Diet) look gourmet. It was literally the cheapest, lowest quality food available. It even made the food at the hospital look edible.

Since I believe that diet can have an effect on health, either positively or negatively, this was unacceptable to me. Also, the group home had this bad smell, and my roommate (who had schizophrenia) would wake me up early every morning frantically talking to himself. After a few weeks, I became suicidal. I did not see a way to a better life. I felt helpless, hopeless, and powerless, and I did not want to go on like that. I took off in my car, an old Subaru my parents had bought me when I had returned to Connecticut. I was the only resident with a car, and when the other group home members first saw it, they looked at me in amazement—like I had this incredibly unfair privilege.

My dad happened to call me on my cell phone, and I told him that I was on my way to buy rope at the hardware store, to then go into the woods and hang myself. Suicide was something I had thought about on and off throughout my illness, but my belief in karma—that I would just have to relive the same lessons over again (and likely worse)—was a strong deterrent. I was put off by the thought of the pain that I would cause my family, and the bad example I would set for my younger brother and other siblings. Also, I don't think I could have gone through with it even if I had wanted to. We have this innate survival instinct inside of us that I don't think I could have overridden (thank God), not to mention the fear of death.

While I don't think that this was my plan or intention, when I told my dad what I was thinking, he immediately told me that I could move back in with him. This option to change my current situation, though it was not ideal, was enough to make me feel a little better. I agreed and went back to the group home to start packing my things. Moving back in with my dad was a step up from the group home, but it was a place that I had been before, and it was still challenging for me.

My father and his then fiancée would ask me every day if I had showered and brushed my teeth. As an adult in my mid-twenties, this made me feel like I was being treated like a child, like I was incapable of taking care of myself. It was the opposite of empowering. Also, they tend to be germaphobes, and certain things in the house had to be wiped down or cleaned after each use. While I am grateful that they took me in, I did not feel comfortable there, and I did not feel like I could be myself.

I got a part-time job at a local pizza restaurant as a waiter. I had waited tables in college and didn't really like it. I didn't like interacting with so many different people. Some of them were quite moody, and I didn't like having to juggle multiple tasks on my plate (no pun intended) at the same time. However, this pizza place had a natural twist, so I reasoned that it was in line with my interests.

I could only work part-time, because there was an income limit on how much I could earn per month while on Social Security disability. They allow for a certain number of months of a trial work period, where you can earn over the limit, but I burned up those months during all of my attempts at employment. It got to the point where if I went to work full-time, I would lose the disability and would be making the same amount as I was when I was working part-time and collecting disability. In order to increase my income, I would not only have to go from part-time to full-time but also get a pay increase as well. This did not create much incentive for me, though I did not plan on living on less than $20,000 gross income per year for the rest of my life. It was a challenge I did not overcome until the fall of 2012.

The following year, in the summer of 2007, I moved across the country to Northern California with a woman I had met about six months earlier and was dating, and I had the opportunity to experience some independence. I tried really hard to get involved in local community activities, jobs, yoga classes, and so forth, but I was still constantly struggling. Everything looked perfect on the outside, but I did not feel happy. I didn't feel like I was being the person I was meant to be. No matter how hard I tried, I could not find my path.

I ended up struggling with food and sex addiction. It seems like during much of that time I was looking at pornography multiple times a day. At one point, I was eating a half-gallon container of Breyer's ice cream per day, in between pornography sessions. Some days I would go out and buy a second container, and I ended up being my heaviest ever at fifty pounds overweight. I felt full of shame and that I was squandering my potential. I was consumed with myself and by my own problems.

This state of self-obsession and addiction without a purpose was like a hell on earth for me. I still didn't feel like my life had started, and my greatest fear was not fulfilling my potential—not being the person I knew I could be. There were days that I would just sit on the porch staring up at the sky and feeling agony for no apparent reason.

I didn't know how to engineer my life into one that I wanted. Just getting by wasn't enough for me. I didn't want to be someone living a "life of quiet desperation," as Henry David Thoreau said. I wanted to be self-actualized, to be fulfilling my dharma, to be doing good. I wanted to be making a difference in the world and have some meaning in my life. I knew that I had it in me. I just didn't know how to live it.

These were poems that I wrote in 2008, during a time I was feeling much despair:

Poems (2008)

Mind
Chaos creating a confused world
But clarity inside gasping for air
My actions do not foretell my future
And yet how can I traverse the jagged path?

Questions whirling a mind into oblivion
Coming back again and again like ripples
Unsettling the calm still waters.
As the stones leave my fingertips.

I'd like to be a tight-rope walker.
How hard dreams are to remember
When they come back to me I don't know
If it is day or it is night.

Someone inside wanting, just wanting
And the actions do not foretell
How can I be the mountain
And move it at the same time?

(March, 2008)

Opportunities Past

This apathy is worse than death
Never leaving the comfort zone
Never growing, turning to stone.

My actions are equivalent to theft
A life that could have been
A life that's full of sin.

At any point I could have left
And to my potential made claim
And gotten rid of all this shame.

(April 5, 2008)

Waiting

Sitting here, it's what I fear
Longing for the past
A feeling I cannot define
Has come to me at last

Sitting here, it's become clear
My dreams are fading fast
And a sense of urgency is what I feel
As time moves slowly past.

(April 5, 2008)

Asleep

Anesthetized, as life passes me by
Stuck in the mud, as hard as I try
So much at stake, you'd think I could cry

What to do, I could not say
Nothing changes, as much as I pray
How could it be, I'm wasting away?

(April 6, 2008)

Hope

Apathy fills the sky
Dark and grey

A bird flies by
I wish it would stay

Take me with you
I think to myself

To where it is blue
But she keeps to herself.

(April 6, 2008)

Alone

This depth of mind
Cannot be communicated.
How can I relate?
No way to show myself,
No way to reveal my state.
Alone in this,
The world seen through my eyes.
I'll talk to the stars,
Maybe they'll surmise.

(April 10, 2008)

Me at fifty pounds overweight; Summer 2008.

A Decade with Mental Illness, Part II

Back in CT Again and the Start of Something Great

After about a year and a half, in late 2008, I told the woman (who I was then engaged to) that I had to leave. She was a wonderful woman, and I enjoyed our time together; however, I wasn't being challenged in the relationship, and I couldn't find happiness there. I had to try something different.

I was initially going to try to ride a bicycle cross-country to get back to Connecticut. I wanted an adventure, to feel alive again. I bought all of this equipment with a cash-advance on my credit card and started bicycling to get in shape. I was planning this whole trip, and everyone was cautioning me against it. I knew that when a person dreams big, sometimes others will try to deflate it. I don't think they do it intentionally. I just think that many people's default operating system is fear (though it doesn't have to be that way).

I ended up scrapping the trip, not because of other people—because if I had wanted it badly enough I would have done it—but mostly because I didn't have the courage to do it; I was afraid, too. So I returned as much of the equipment that I had bought as I could, and with the little bit of money I had left, I bought a tiny, old $1,200 Honda beater that had been impounded and never claimed. I loaded up my personal belongings and started the drive to head back east. The car was literally filled to the roof with my stuff, so that I could barely see out the windows. It also had a problem where if the gas tank fell below halfway, it would stall, so I had to stop twice as frequently to fill up with gas.

One of my friends from high school had a spare room in his four-bedroom apartment near downtown New Haven, and I thought that a city would be a good place to get a job and get involved. I moved in there right when I got back to Connecticut. I had already been tapering down my medication a little during my time in California. Since the medication made me feel dull, lethargic, and a little numb all over, I blamed it in part for my inability to fulfill my potential. I felt like I was only half alive when taking it and didn't think that I could ever feel fulfilled like that. I didn't know how I could ever live the rest of my life half-alive. I often thought that I would rather die than live an unfulfilled life. So I took the risk again, and on January 1st, 2009, I decided to try going off of my medication for the second time.

While at my friend's apartment in New Haven, I wasn't getting any traction with anything. I would sit in the apartment alone all day looking for jobs online while everyone else was at work. My situation looked bleak, I felt heavy, and I didn't feel like I had the energy required to reach "escape velocity," defined by the *Merriam-Webster* dictionary as: the minimum velocity that a moving body must have to escape from the gravitational field of a celestial body and move outward into space. It felt like my illness had this "weight" over me that was holding me back, and I didn't have the energy required to break free.

After about one month in the New Haven area, I decided to move back to my parents' area of the state. I knew that it would not be good for me if I lived at either of my parents' houses, so I was looking for a small, inexpensive, one-bedroom apartment or studio. My mother helped me find a little apartment in town for about $550 per month. At this point, after five years, my disability income was probably around $800 per month (it went up every year). This meant that I could cover most of my home expenses with the disability income, and I would need to work part-time to cover food, gas, and other expenses. I got a job working part-time in another warehouse, packing orders for shipping.

Around this same time, I contacted the local yoga studio to see if I could volunteer. I had long had the desire to teach yoga, and I wanted to go for it. (I had taken a week-long teacher training program in 2007). The studio owner was partnered with a holistic business in the same location. When I got to the studio to discuss volunteering teaching yoga, I also met the two women who were running the holistic business. I immediately had an affinity for them. When interacting with one of the women in particular, Katherine, I felt more energetic and more alive. They brought out a playful side in me that I hadn't seen in a while, and we immediately became friends.

I found it difficult to teach yoga with the low energy and fatigue I was still experiencing, and I wasn't attracting any students. My one-bedroom apartment was nice but somewhat isolating. When my newfound friends from the holistic center weren't available to hang out, I had nothing to do on the weekends. I remember on Friday night, Saturday, or Sunday, I felt like I had too much time on my hands, and I didn't know what to do with myself.

There were some days that I would sit on my sofa and stare at the wall for what seemed like hours. I had some independence, which was good, but I still felt like I was wasting my life without purpose. I started researching online natural health certificate programs, so that I could begin meaningful work, and I enrolled in a program. I also signed up for another yoga teacher training program. I was going to go for it once again!

My Second Relapse

By the end of September of that year, I started to experience symptoms again (which for the second time, started about nine months after going off my medication). As with the previous relapse, within a matter of days I was having a full-blown psychotic episode. I was feeling affected by the energy of the people and environment around me. I was too wired to sleep, and I was losing control fast.

After about a week—in early October, after my twenty-ninth birthday dinner with my family—I lay in bed with my mind racing. I thought that I was dying again and made the wise decision to call for an ambulance. After getting inside of it and onto the stretcher, I lost consciousness, just as I had the previous two times. I came to inside the hospital, and the EMT was really straining to push the stretcher down the hall. I thought that I was so close to death that my energy was tremendously heavy for some reason. The stretcher stopped against the wall just past the nurse's station in the emergency room, and the EMT sighed and said "Good luck" with a worrisome shrug of his eyebrows. Then he turned and walked away.

I lay there on the stretcher feeling about as terrible as you could imagine feeling, and I felt like I had nothing left. I wanted to be contributing, to be of service to society in some way, but I couldn't even take care of myself. I was smelling that bad smell that I often experienced during my psychotic episodes; it smelled like death. There was a woman in a nearby room (off of the hall) crying and a man consoling her, and I thought that maybe she had cancer and that I was smelling her dying.

Around that time, I had been listening to a yogic chant album and one of the songs, when referring to a Hindu god, said, "He swallowed up the poison and saved the whole world." As I lay there feeling helpless and hopeless, I thought that the only way I could give back would be to take in other people's suffering. In some weird act of martyrdom and self-sacrifice, I breathed in that death smell and thought that I was taking the sickness away from the woman in the nearby room.

My adrenaline kicked in again after a few minutes of laying there, and I started feeling more alert and anxious. I got up from the stretcher and walked up to the nurse's station. The affect on my face must have looked flat, and I was trying to get the nurse's attention. She said, "Hey, Hollywood" with a little bit of a rude tone. I interpreted that as her saying that I was seeking attention, like a Hollywood star. Here I was trying to give everything that I had, and she thought I was trying to take. This lack of understanding—in her not seeing the real me—hurt me deeply.

I walked back to my stretcher and laid down. After a while, I was rolled into the locked psych section of the emergency room and given a bed. I was freezing cold, and one of the nurses brought me a warm blanket and wrapped it around me. It felt so good for someone to care like that. I laid in bed feeling the warmth and actually felt a little at peace. It was a long night in there waiting to get a room up on the seventh floor. I would get up from time to time and walk around the small main room, go to the bathroom, or look through the windows of the locked doors into the ER, or into the small nurse's station adjoined to this particular wing. Then I would go back to bed and curl up.

At one point, a janitorial woman who looked Eastern European came in to clean the main area, to which the four or five patient rooms were attached. I walked up to her and asked if I could help her. I still had this innate desire to be of service. She looked at me with a scared expression on her face and said "You want to help me?" I had the white blanket wrapped around my shoulders, and

I was holding it closed in front of my neck. My face must have looked pale and gaunt from the weight I had lost, and the blanket could have looked like a cape. I thought that she thought I looked like Dracula and that she was afraid. This thought terrified me. She said that I didn't need to help, so I went back to my bed and laid down again.

Once up on the seventh floor, I was incredibly on edge. I remember there was an older stocky man who was an alcoholic and had been recently admitted after a binge. When he breathed, I felt like his mouth was an energy vortex, sucking energy from me. One day he and I and one other person were moving a folding table away from the center of the group room, so that we could have our daily support group session. We were not working together and were straining in different directions to move the table up against the wall.

When we finally placed it there, the older man took a deep breath, and I felt a twinge in my heart and saw a flash of red (what I thought was blood) shoot out of my chest and up his nose. Then I saw him "fart" it onto the chair behind him. Terrified, I went up to a nurse and told her there was blood on the chair. She promptly came in and took the chair out of the room. That was just one of the many crazy, terrifying experiences that I endured during this psychotic episode, as well as during the previous ones. Suffice it to say, it was no fun.

Dating my Future Wife

After discharge, I tried to go back to my old routine. I still had my one-bedroom apartment in town and my part-time job. However, I was now back on medication, feeling incredibly beat-up and weak, and I had to start the rehabilitation process of rebuilding my life once again. I continued to push through the difficulties as best I could, like I had been doing over the previous seven years.

That winter, I was hanging out with my friend Katherine at her apartment, and we were doing horoscope compatibility profiles online for people we knew, just for fun. We would plug in the information for one friend paired with another to see how compatible they were. At one point, I suggested she try her and I, just to see. We entered in our information, and the results screen popped up showing "100 percent compatible." This was the first time we had seen this number.

Though this was just a silly game, I think it helped spark the seed that was already in our minds that we wanted to be more than just friends. After a few conversations about it during the following days, we decided to give it a try and go on our first date. We went on our first date that January, and it was obvious there was a romantic connection between us.

I was also hospitalized in the inpatient unit for a medication adjustment that month—not great timing when starting a new relationship. However, Katherine visited me up on the seventh floor, facing her fear of being trapped in elevators; ironically, she got stuck in the elevator on the way down for about twenty minutes. While we did have almost a year's friendship under our belts, the fact that she visited me in the hospital was significant to me.

Later, during our first year of dating, she would tell me that she could "see the real me" and that she could "see how great I was" through the illness. While I normally did better in a relationship than alone, having a partner who saw me, believed in me, and was supportive of my condition was immeasurably helpful to me. She was like a rock in my life and something to work for. In addition to that, she was also the one who found the thing that would ultimately heal me. Needless to say, she was and is one of the greatest blessings in my life.

By mid-2010, I was still struggling at work and having a difficult time coping with the stress. At some point I had to stop. I decided that I would apply for and move into low-income subsidized housing, so that I would not be at risk of losing my residence. I was accepted, and in June moved into a small one-bedroom apartment in a large building complex. The halls of the building smelled really bad, and some of the other residents would hang outside during the day smoking cigarettes.

Like the group home, this place felt like somewhat of a resting home. I was still fighting to get better and was trying to do things to help myself. I would go for jogs, and as I was leaving the building, some of the other residents would look at me like I was from another planet. I am amazed that Katherine stood by me through this time. She even weathered the smelly building and the uncomfortable gazes of the other residents to come visit me there. After six months of this, Katherine agreed that I could move in with her. Thankfully, my employer was somewhat understanding of my condition, and I was able to get my job back.

Katherine and I went through our first few years not without challenges. I still felt incredibly numbed and fatigued from the medication, and I had some emotional instability and anger (which I attributed to the injustice of my illness that I felt I had endured). We broke up and got back together a number of times, and those years were still a tremendous struggle for me. Nonetheless, in the fall of 2012, my part-time work had been going well for about a year, and I decided to go to full-time.

I was able to get a promotion at work and go to full-time employment, and so that month my Social Security disability ended. After eight years of being dependant on the system, I was finally free. I was finally supporting myself without government aid (though the Medicare did not end until two years after the disability ended, based on the law). However, while I was able to function at this point, I still felt that my life was missing meaning and purpose. I still felt somewhat numb, not fully "alive," and I wasn't truly fulfilled.

Finding Healing: Homeopathy

In late 2012, Katherine was researching schizoaffective disorder online and commenting on how there were surprisingly few stories about recovery. She was looking for a cure and stumbled upon a naturopathic doctor who treats mental illness solely with homeopathy. Homeopathy is a system of medicine based on the principle that "like cures like," a concept which dates back to Hippocrates, the father of medicine.

I didn't know much about it, but I thought it was worth a try. I called the doctor, Dr. Mark Janikula, for my initial phone consultation, and he seemed confident that he could help me, so I scheduled my initial intake appointment for January of 2013. One of the beautiful things about homeopathy is that it doesn't have any side effects, and he was able to begin treating me while I was still on pharmaceutical medication.

His office was in California, so I flew out for my first appointment. I flew out alone and had to rent a car and stay in a hotel in an unknown city all by myself. This was definitely outside of my comfort zone, but the chance at healing was important enough to me to push through it. I met with Dr. Janikula for four hours as he took my medical history, asked me all about my life and my symptoms, and asked about any other information that would be useful to him.

He gave me a general overview of homeopathy and how it worked. As far as I understand it, a homeopathic remedy is matched with a specific set of symptoms. The substance that the remedy is made from is one that would normally cause those symptoms in a person. The remedy is made by taking that substance and repeatedly diluting and shaking it in water, until at some point the original substance is no longer present. When taken, the remedy triggers the body to come back into balance. I see it as a form of energy medicine, as if the water used to make a remedy maintains an energetic remnant of the original substance, that then stimulates the body to heal itself.

At the end of the session, Dr. Janikula already knew which remedy I needed, one that matched the symptoms of my illness very well. Before I left, he gave me my remedy, a small glass vile with little white pellets in it. I was to dissolve three pellets under my tongue once a day. I flew back home feeling a small sense of hope. At least I had a plan and was taking action to feel better.

I was able to do future appointments after that by phone. When my symptoms stopped improving or started getting worse, Dr. Janikula would either change the potency of my remedy or switch me to a different remedy. By June of that year, just six months later, I was feeling much better. During this time, I was still seeing my prescribing psychiatrist and had kept him informed of my working with the naturopathic doctor and taking homeopathy. Luckily, he was somewhat open-minded to me trying harmless alternative treatments, though he probably didn't think it would work.

I wanted to stop the pharmaceutical medication, as I still attributed some of my remaining symptoms to it. Dr. Janikula said that I didn't have to stop them yet, that he could continue treating me while I was on the medication, but it was really important to me and I felt I was ready. By the end of June of 2013 I had weaned myself off the pharmaceutical medication (under his supervision), for the last time.

As a side note, I believe that one of the major stumbling blocks to health in America is the fact that our current health care system is a for-profit system. One of the drugs that I was taking for my psychosis, called Abilify, cost $300 for a month's supply (as seen on my insurance statement at the time). My homeopathic remedy costs $8 for a month's supply. Since the main objective of a drug company is to make profit—not to get people well—this is an inherent, unavoidable conflict of interest.

The healthier people are, the less medication they would need—but to make more money a drug company needs to sell *more* medication. This conflict of interest of a profit-based system contributes to tremendous human suffering and is inhibiting humanity from moving forward in health. I pray that humanity is shifting toward a more purpose-driven mentality, where we hold the well-being of people and the planet above making money.

Now, the past two times that I had stopped my medication, it took around nine months for my symptoms to come back with a fury. Within a couple of days they would be full-blown, and I would land in the hospital within a week or two. The difference this time was that I was being treated with homeopathy and doing it under a doctor's supervision. Nonetheless, about eight months after stopping my medication, in February of 2014, I began noticing some symptoms returning during a twenty-four-hour period.

My sleep had also started to be affected the night or two before. I was in the grocery store, and I started feeling like the energy of my surroundings was moving through me. Katherine also noticed that my face didn't look right, and thankfully we had the wisdom to call my doctor. Dr. Janikula called me back that evening and switched my remedy. The next day my symptoms lessened and I felt a little better, and the day after that my symptoms were gone. That was over two years ago, and that was the last time I experienced symptoms to that degree.

At this point, I have been symptom-free for over two years and medication and side-effect-free for over two and a half years. I am still taking a homeopathic remedy daily, and I check in with my doctor once every few months. At some point, as he explained to me, I won't have to take remedies or talk to him anymore in regard to my past illness. However, I will still take homeopathic remedies for any other health conditions I might face, as it has proven its worth to me.

Happy and healthy again; November 2014.

Universal Principles for Healing

How Did I Heal?

Since getting better, I've often reflected on the meaning of my illness and how I healed. If I had to narrow it down to three main factors that contributed to my healing, they would be the following:

1. Having a loving, supportive partner who believes in me.
2. The healing power of homeopathy.
3. My spiritual outlook.

Number one is largely outside of our control, though the growth work that we do on ourselves can help attract the right partner to us and help us to maintain a healthy relationship. I believe that if there is someone out there who is meant for us, we'll find that person.

Number two is a simple choice that is largely within our control. You just have to find a skilled homeopath to work with. (You can refer to my website, healingschizoaffective. com, for resources about homeopathy.) Homeopathy is side-effect free and relatively inexpensive, so why not give it a try?

Homeopathy works. I know that there are some naysayers out there who will say it is not scientific. My response to that is that the purpose of true science is not to uphold the status quo of beliefs but to discover what is possible. A scientist is a neutral observer who is open-minded and devoted to observing and understanding the truth. Just because some current mainstream scientists don't understand (or don't want to understand) homeopathy, doesn't mean that it doesn't work. As I've often said to people whose belief systems won't budge, would you rather be right or would you rather that you, your loved one, or your patients be healed? I'm not going to say much more to make the case for homeopathy, because I feel that my story is compelling enough. The choice is yours!

Number three, our spiritual outlook is 100 percent within our control. It is this essential part of my healing journey that I will elaborate on here.

100 Percent Accountability and Free Will

My yoga teacher once said, "There is a difference between wanting to change the world and wanting to change the world to make your life easier." I used to have so much anger toward society—the way it was structured, and the people who supported it or were content being oblivious to it. I thought that the egoic systems in place were to the detriment to the betterment of humanity. While that may have been true, my anger was not serving the world or me.

I got to a point where I realized that I had to take 100 percent personal accountability for my life and myself. I couldn't blame society or anyone else for my problems. I had heard of the book, *Man's Search for Meaning*, by Viktor Frankl, where even in the confines of a holocaust concentration camp, he realized that he was free. He realized that he was free to choose how he reacted to his situation. That freedom is there for all of us. The truth is, the only thing that we have control over is that which we have control over, just like the message of the Serenity Prayer. Everything else is besides the point.

Once I truly began to accept my free will and the power of my own choices, I started to trade in blame, anger, and resentment for empowerment. It was exciting to know that I am 100 percent responsible for my own life and that no one else has this power over me. This simple shift in perspective is life-changing. It was tempting to use my illness as a crutch, but I realized that if my life were going to improve, it would be by my own actions.

I became like a neutral researcher, evaluating my choices and their effects on my life. My main criteria was that I wanted to move in the direction of healing. Beyond that, I dropped the dogma of certain beliefs. If they weren't serving me, I let them go. If I were a vegetarian, and eating some meat helped improve my life—or vice versa—so be it. If working out at the gym wasn't serving me, but going for hikes in nature was, so be it. In essence, I placed less value in my "mental programming"—the way I had been conditioned to think over my lifetime—and more value on what worked.

Ultimately, I realized that I am a steward of my own life, and while I am responsible for it, it is ultimately borrowed. I am a vehicle for the life force to work through me. This alleviated a lot of my guilt and self-blame. It didn't matter if I had been bad or was to blame for my current situation. What mattered was only that I grew toward goodness from that point forward. In that way, I could take responsibility for my life but with a sense of detachment. If I made a poor choice, rather than beating myself up about it, I saw it as an opportunity to make a correction.

Through taking ownership of my own life, while also letting go of the guilt, my higher purpose became larger than myself. I was working to be a better person, for myself and the world. I was working to be in alignment with the life force and the Creator. My "mission" became larger than my own problems, and this was incredibly freeing for me. It stopped being "all about me" and started being about something greater. This gave me a renewed sense of meaning, a shared purpose, and a feeling of collaboration and cooperation with the universe.

Faith in an Infinite, Loving Creator

I would say that faith in an infinite, loving creator, or at least in some higher benevolent power, is the number one spiritual choice essential to healing. I frame my every experience around this knowing. If something I don't like happens to me, I think to myself that it happened so I could learn a lesson, and therefore it is in my highest good. If I see evil in the world, I think to myself that it exists to challenge humanity to grow and fulfill our potential. I know that the laws of our universe are designed for our benefit.

Take the law of cause and effect, for example. We know that if we stick our hand in a fire, we'll get burned. This is a predictable and stable law. We may think that this "consequence" is not in our best interest, but I see the predictability of this law as kind. Would you rather live in a universe without cause and effect, where one day you stick your hand in a fire and get burned, and the next day it feels like a gentle caress? That would be true chaos!

It's not that the fire is trying to harm us; it's just an expression of life that is following the natural laws. If we learn to work within the framework of the natural laws and align ourselves with them rather than trying to fight against them, we can experience all of the magnificence that this life has to offer. The fact that natural laws exist is proof enough to me of a greater intelligence than ourselves, and I know that the natural laws are for our own good and are designed for our evolution toward wholeness.

Even in my darkest moments, when I had lost faith that I would get better and was angry because I could not see a way out, I still knew on some level that there is more to life than just me and the material world. Without this spiritual context, it would just be every man or woman for him or herself. What would be the point of everything? What would be our motivation to grow and to heal?

Though the relief of pain is a powerful motivator, self-indulgence was not reason enough for me.

Knowing that there is a greater power outside of my control and that it is all-loving was a source of comfort and strength for me. The beautiful thing is that spirituality is a choice. We can choose to believe that the circumstances we are going through are for our highest good, even if we can't see how at the moment. We can choose to believe that the universe and the laws that govern it are innately good. We can choose to make learning to love our personal mission in life. We can choose to believe in an infinitely intelligent, infinitely loving creator or source. That is ultimate freedom.

Healing is Possible

Another choice that we have is to believe that healing is possible. Life moves toward vibrance, wholeness, balance, and healing—and we are no different. While we have been taught that illness is some external force waging war on us, we can choose to reframe our understanding to one with purpose—namely, that illness is an imbalance in the body and that symptoms are intended to warn and heal us.

In the case of a fever when we have a cold, our body is raising our core temperature in an attempt to kill off an infection and to alert us that we are ill. This causes us to slow down, rest, and take better care of ourselves. Mental illness can be a sign of serious imbalances in our lives and can lead us to seek balance and wholeness.

If we believe that healing is possible, that alone will increase our chances of healing. New advances in science are confirming what spirituality has known for thousands of years, that our beliefs affect our reality. Quantum mechanics has shown us that the observer of an experiment affects the outcome of the experiment.

This is the cause of the placebo effect, which is more than just some anomaly to be controlled for in experiments. It is real. (I am mentioning this to make the case for the belief in healing, *not* to relate it to homeopathy; homeopathy is not the same as taking any old sugar pill and is definitely more than just the placebo effect, as evidenced by the fact that it works on babies and pets.) Our intention to heal and the knowledge that it is possible will actually promote healing. It may not happen in the time frame that we would like, but I believe that if we desire something strongly enough, are persistent enough with it over time, and our intentions are pure (and in alignment with the natural laws), then we can eventually achieve it.

Knowing that healing is possible is more than just a belief. It is a model or framework for seeing and understanding the world. If we look at nature and see harmony and balance, then we know that we are also a part of that. However, if we look at nature and see ruthless competition, then we will operate from that reference point instead.

Our "personal philosophy" or worldview will change how we respond to situations, and how we play the game of life. That is why it is so important to consider from what reference point we are coming from and to reflect on our personal values and beliefs. We will often find that a belief that we hold dear was given to us by a parent, a teacher, or by society—something we placed our authority in—and may not even be true for us.

This is particularly true for health. The current mainstream medical model doesn't even recognize the existence of a life force, which is the true source of health, whereas other more holistic models do. But that is all they are, just models. If we choose to buy into one model at the exclusion of another, it can limit our options and our outcome. It can lead us to believe that healing is not possible or that a specific treatment is our only option.

Remember, we are ultimately responsible for ourselves and our own health. If we choose to place our trust and authority in one doctor or another, that is still our choice, and we are lending that person our power to make a decision for us. However, we are each individually responsible for our own lives and our own health!

This does not mean that we can control every external event but rather that we can control that which we have control over, and we can choose how we react to those events. Like Viktor Frankl in the concentration camp, we still have our free will regardless of circumstance. I've been involuntarily committed on more than one occasion. In the psych unit in the ER, I was legally not able to refuse medication, and one time I was given the choice between taking a pill or being restrained and given an injection.

I chose to go with the pill, but I also chose to believe that that person couldn't touch my soul. He could affect my body at that moment, but he couldn't affect my spirit or who I was inside. He couldn't affect my destiny. That was wholly up to me!

The Transformative Power of Meditation

Meditation is one of the most powerful transformational tools available. It connects us to our true selves, our higher selves, and to the divine. It raises our consciousness to a place where meaning and purpose exist, where life is in perspective, and to where we are able to live authentically.

Meditation is not something that can be forced with the will. There are days when it will feel great and days when it is hard to sit still or concentrate. The important thing is to just do it. Do it when you are feeling good, and do it when you are not. When practiced daily with consistency, its benefits add up over time to create powerful shifts in our lives.

It's like saving a few dollars each day in a savings account with compound interest. At some point, you will be abundantly wealthy. However, the wealth of meditation is not just financial freedom; it is the ability to be true to yourself, to be less reactive and affected by external situations, to see life with a deeper clarity, and most importantly, to have a greater capacity to love.

There was a time during my illness when I was unable to meditate. My mind was too unsettled, and it would actually become more perturbed if I tried to meditate. Also, when I was on pharmaceutical medication, the dullness that I felt behind my forehead made meditation difficult for me. In instances such as these, if you are not able to practice seated meditation, doing an activity with intentional awareness can have similar positive benefits.

For example, practicing some form of physical exercise such as yoga or tai chi, while maintaining awareness of the physical sensations of the body and the breath, is a form of meditation in motion. Other activities, such as cooking or gardening while observing your experience (are you fully present, seeing, and feeling the sensations of the activity, or is your mind someplace else?), are also forms of meditation. Also, listening to sounds in nature or observing nature can be another very effective way to ground yourself and get present.

The object is not to force any specific state but rather to simply be aware of your state, without judgement. Since the life force is good—and ultimately serves us in a way that is best for us—simple awareness with a pure intention will move us in the right direction. It is important not to judge your experience or yourself. Through acceptance and surrender, we can let go of the "baggage" that we carry around with us and free the truth within ourselves.

Living a conscious life is one of the greatest callings that we can answer. The beautiful thing is that what is in our own benefit, or what is good for us, is also what is good for the world. As we grow into more enlightened people, we can have a more positive impact on those around us and the entire planet as a whole.

A Good Life with Purpose

After discontinuing the pharmaceutical medication in June of 2013, while taking homeopathic remedies under the care of my naturopathic doctor, my life just kept getting better and better. I continued working full-time, excelling at work, and my salary more than doubled. Katherine and I were married in late 2014, and shortly after that we bought our first home. I have been maintaining a regular yoga and meditation practice for over a year now, which is something that I deeply wanted to do but was unable to the entire time I was sick.

I feel alive again. I am in touch with my desire to grow, and I feel connected spiritually. During so much of my illness, I was paralyzed by fear. I was afraid of people, places, and things. Now that I feel I am in the clear, I have realized that love was, and is, the antidote. Love is what we are made of, what drives us, and what we are seeking. Any beliefs we have that are not in alignment with love—or the expansion of our capacity to love—are the true delusions.

As I'm sure many people experience, now that I am feeling good again my greatest desire is to give back and to be of service to humanity. Though I had wanted to help others and contribute during my illness, I was unable to, as I wasn't even able to take care of myself. Just like the analogy of putting the oxygen mask on yourself first on an airplane before assisting the person next to you, I had to get on stable enough ground first before I could help others. You can't give what you don't have.

At the end of *Schindler's List*, after spending his entire fortune to save over a thousand lives, Mr. Schindler cries that he could have done more and saved even one more life, and he asks himself if he did enough. I believe that each one of us will have to face the truth within ourselves and answer that same question. There are countless people suffering in the world today, just like during the Holocaust, while many others are consumed by things like shopping and consumption. I don't fault them, because I know that this is due to a lack of awareness. We are all seeking fulfillment, and if people knew that the true source of fulfillment is giving freely of ourselves, all of humanity would be sharing in that beautiful intention. We'll get there!

Nowadays, the projects I am working on to raise consciousness and serve humanity are what get me out of bed in the morning. They are what motivate me when I am tired or uncomfortable and what give me a sense of purpose. I have realized that service to others is the real path to fulfillment and that learning to love is our mission here on Earth.

TEN SPIRITUAL SURVIVAL TIPS TO OVERCOME MENTAL ILLNESS

1. *Adapt* – if what you're doing isn't working, try shifting your perspective. Humans are like lotus flowers; we can grow in the mud. Strive to thrive in your situation, even if it is not ideal.

2. *Seek balance* – health is a state of balance. When our bodily systems are working together in harmony, we experience vibrant health. Our bodies are constantly working to achieve this. Do things regularly that help it achieve balance.

3. *Follow your intuition* – this is your inner knowing that is not based in fear. Intuition just feels right, because it is right. It is a higher guidance that can help lead our way.

4. *Practice daily* – a daily spiritual practice reminds us of our truth and brings us back to our path, again and again. Like saving in a spiritual piggy bank, it builds up our momentum toward the life we want.

5. *Find teachers who inspire you* – people who inspire us have qualities we want to emulate and passions that are in line with our own. They can be contemporary or historical figures who expand our idea of what's possible and inspire us to be better than we are.

6. *Know it's not your fault* – you're doing the best you can, just like everyone else. We don't know why we experience certain challenges, but we do know that we can use them to learn and grow from. Letting go of self-blame and guilt serves our own growth as well as our ability to do good in the world.

7. *Don't use your illness as a crutch* – it may seem easy to blame the illness for your problems and use it as an excuse for not living the life that you desire, but that approach doesn't help you. Not using it as an excuse is a far more empowering approach.

8. *Adjust your timeline* – when we're suffering, of course we want it to end today! However, healing is a process. Practice patience, and recognize that

it takes time. It may not happen in the time frame that you want, but it will happen in God's time.

9. ***Learn to love*** – life is about learning to love, and love is all there is. Rather than becoming embittered or resentful, use each experience as an opportunity to expand your capacity to love. Acceptance and forgiveness are powerful tools in this regard.

10. ***Trust in a higher power*** – Though we may not see all of the reasons for our suffering, have faith that it is happening for a reason. Trust that there is a lesson to be learned or some growth process that we are meant to go through. Know that there's a divine process at work that is in our own best interest.

Conclusion

If you are suffering with schizoaffective disorder or any other mental illness, I hope this story has given you hope. I've been there. I know the unspeakable pain and suffering that mental illness can bring. I know the fear and the feelings of powerlessness it can create. I know the piercing loneliness and the sorrow.

Just know that you are not alone. There are millions of people in the world suffering in the same way. These are people with hopes and dreams just like you, who are also giving all they've got to get better. There are also countless practitioners who deeply care and who are fighting to help people heal.

Despite what some may think, schizoaffective disorder is not a life sentence. I healed from my illness, and so can you! I am no different than you are. I have the same power of choice that you do and the same life force flowing through me. I have a God-given purpose for my life, as do you.

You wouldn't be in the situation that you're in if it weren't meant to be, if you didn't have lessons to learn, or if it weren't for your highest good. Have faith, and persist beyond what you thought possible. Be stronger and more forgiving than you thought possible. Let go of the fear, and fill that space with love instead. Meet the universe halfway, and trust that the rest will fall into place, eventually. God bless you! You are a true spiritual warrior.

To the loved ones of people suffering with mental illness, I know that it is not easy for you either. I witnessed the suffering that my illness caused my family and friends. I know that you are doing your best, and you feel the hurt alongside your loved one. I hope that my story has given you some insight into what your loved one may be experiencing or feeling and some hope that healing is possible. God bless you!

For any health care practitioners who work with mental illness, I salute you. I witnessed the doctors, nurses, psych-techs, and therapists who truly care, working every day in the trenches to help people who are suffering. I know that you are doing your best and working with the tools you have to help get your patients better. You do make a difference! I hope that this book has given you hope as well and maybe shifted your perspective of mental illness in a positive direction, if even just a little bit. God bless you, and keep up the good work!